Art Deco Patterns I

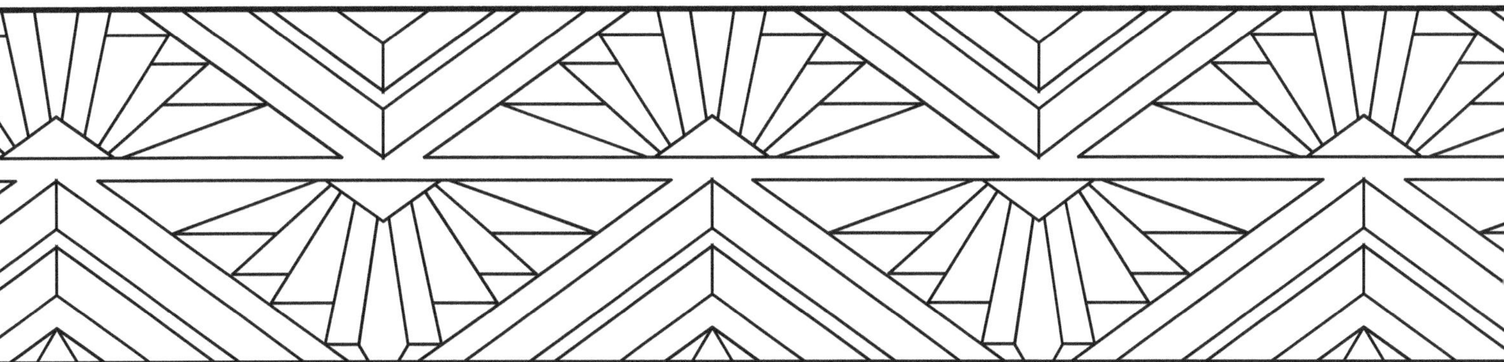

ILLUSTRATIONS BY JULIANNA KUNSTLER

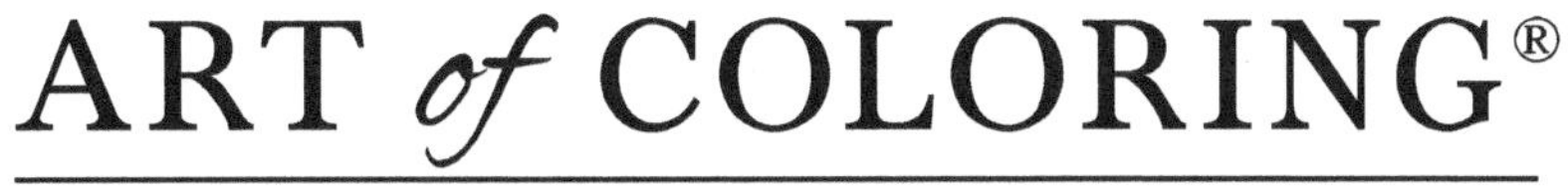

www.juliannakunstler.com

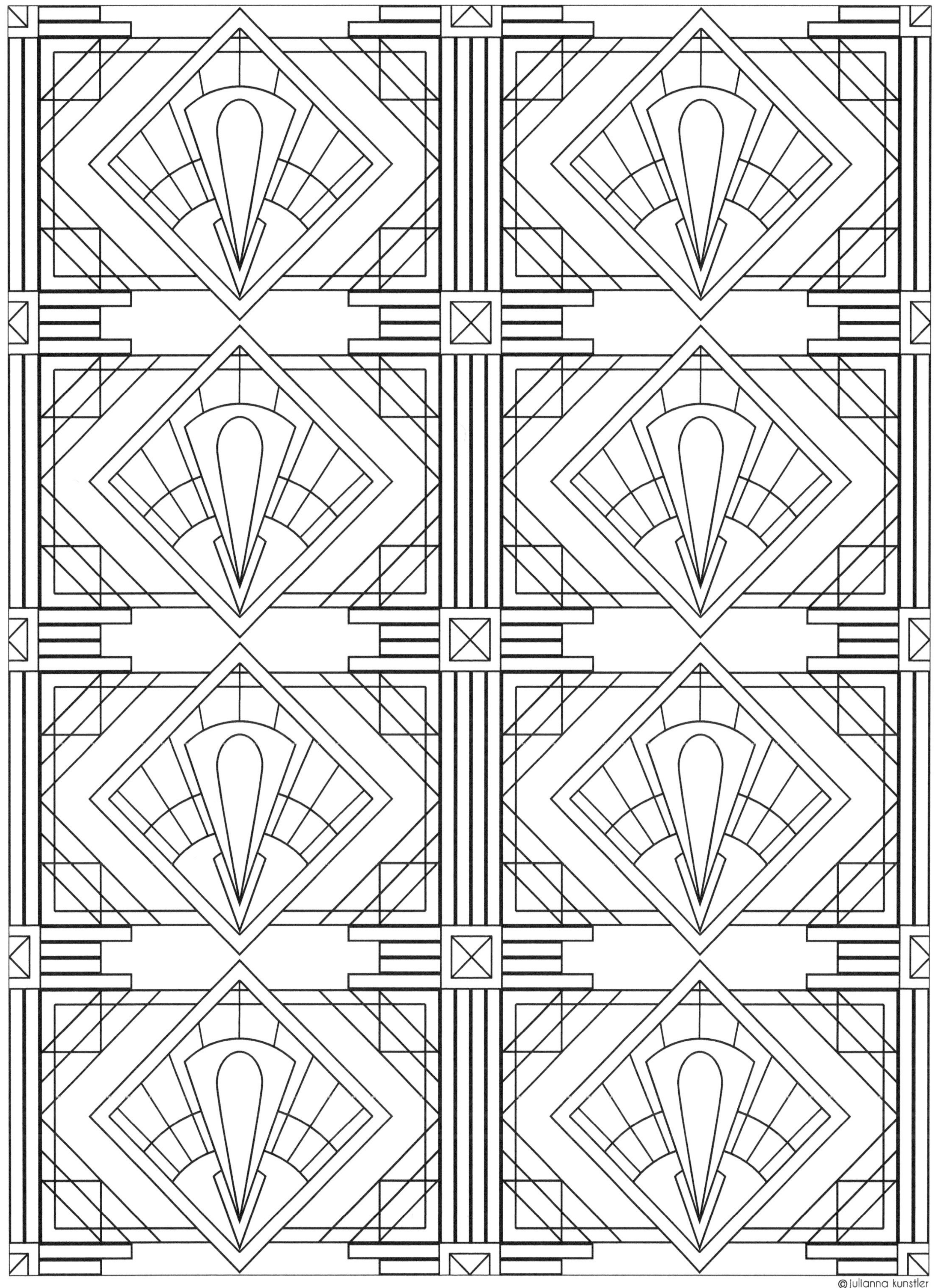

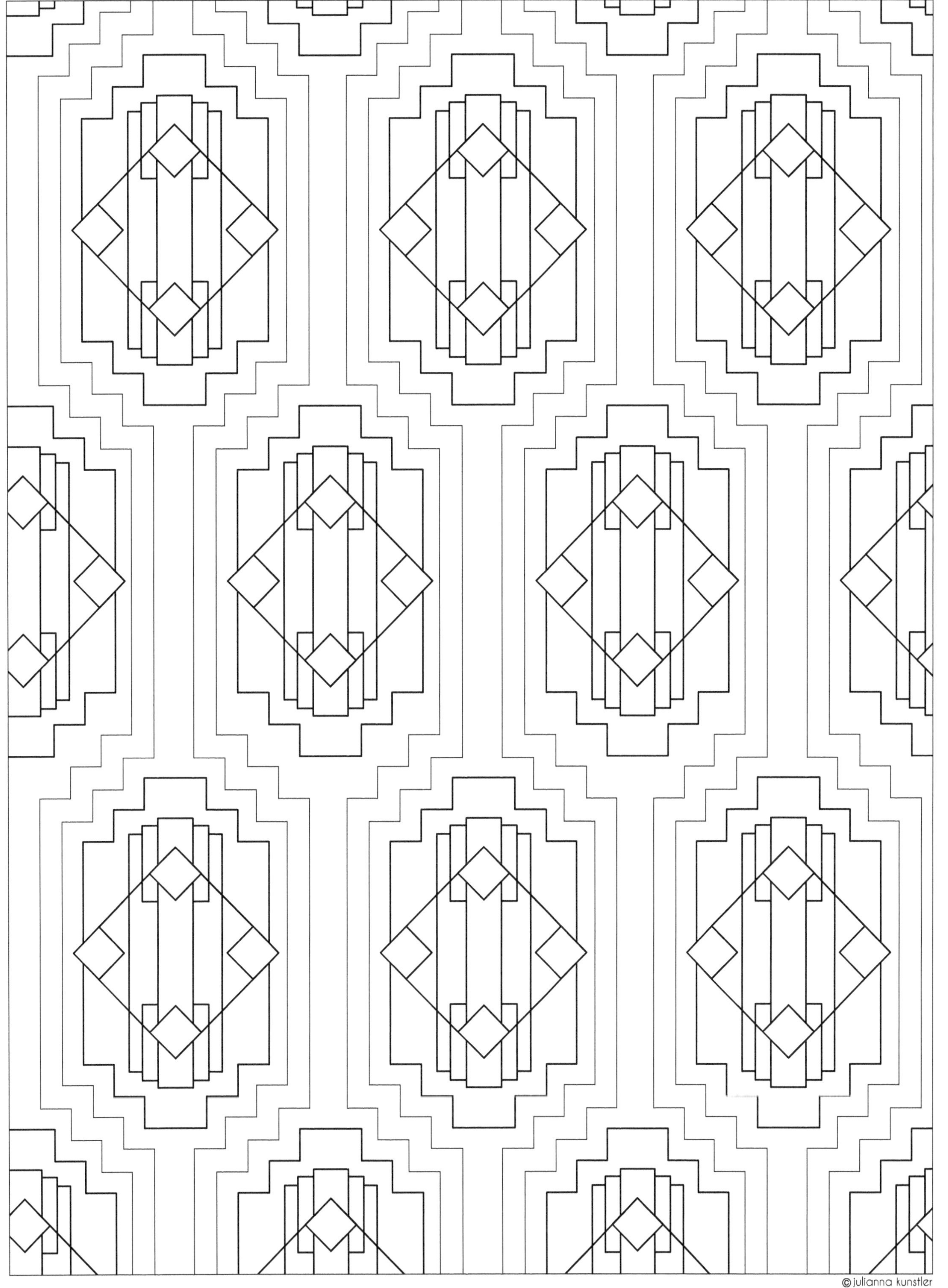

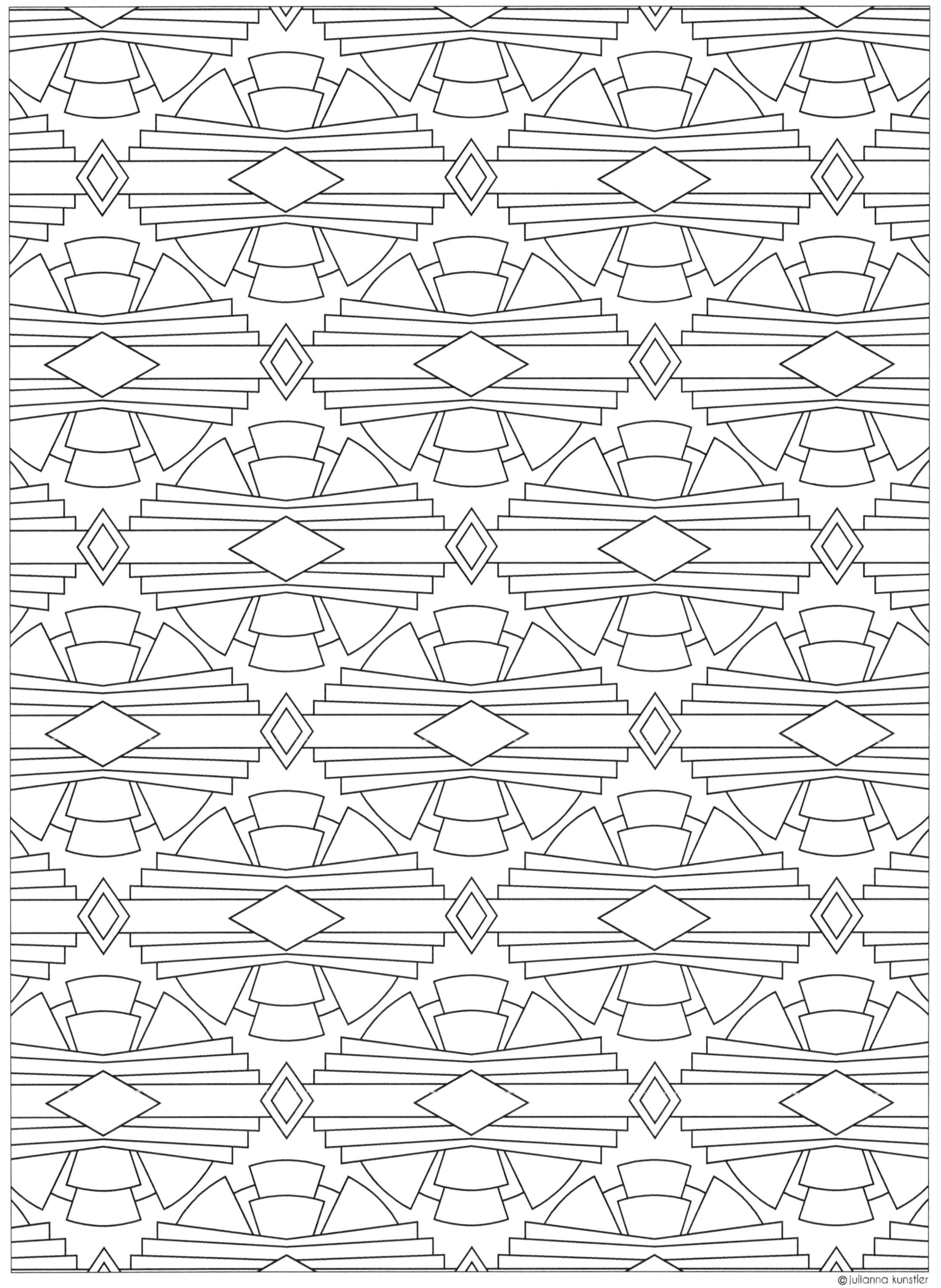

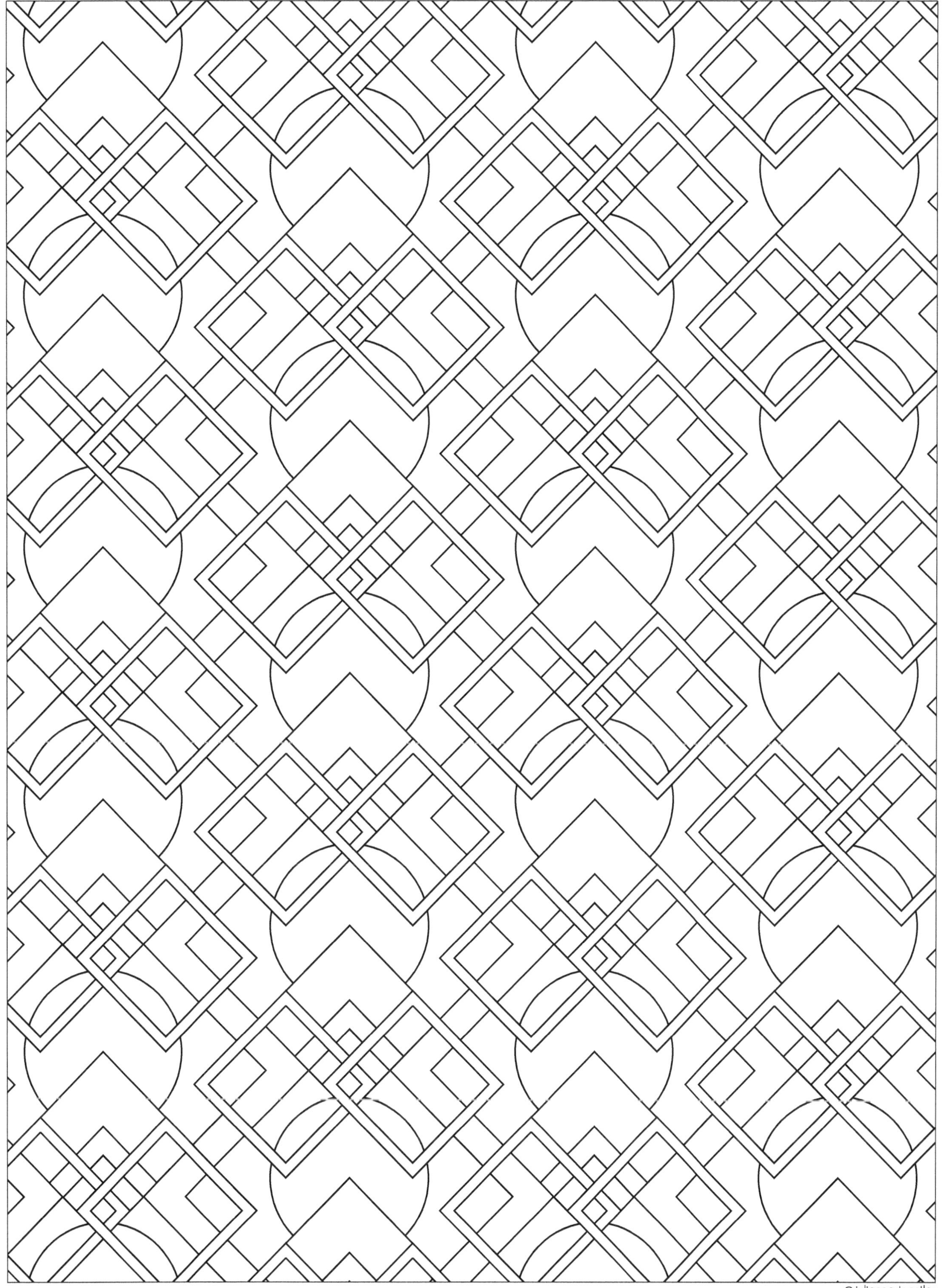

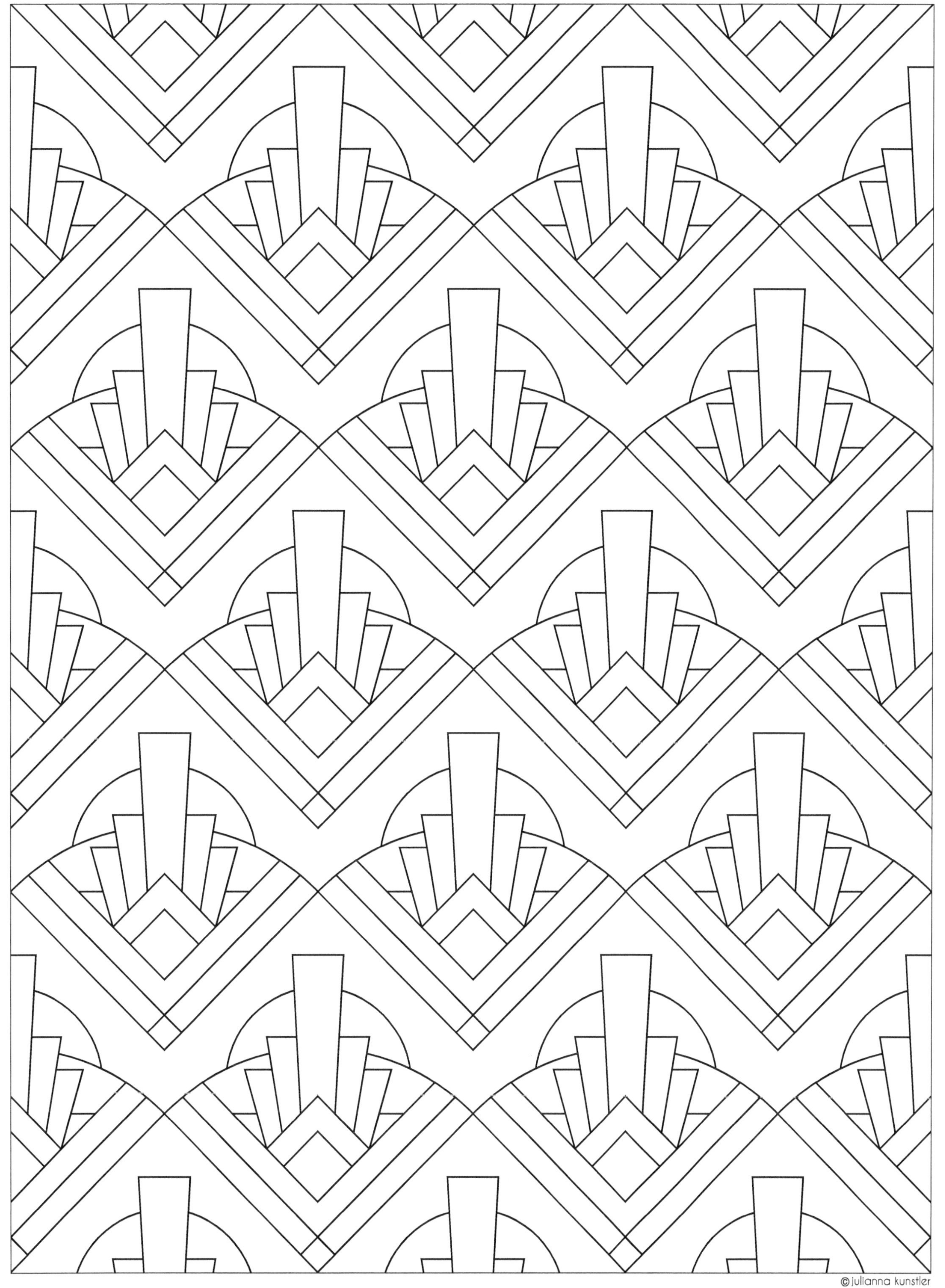

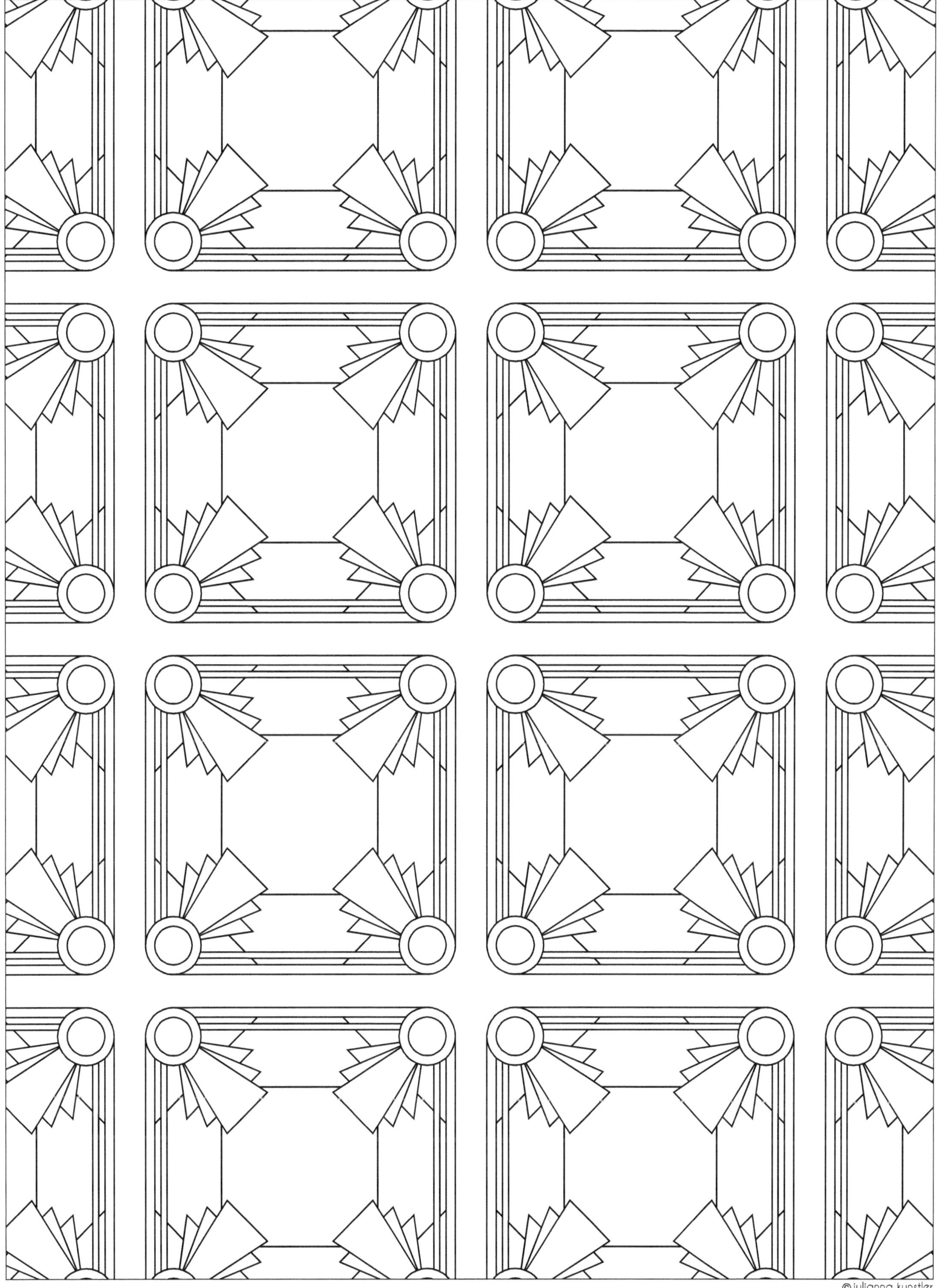

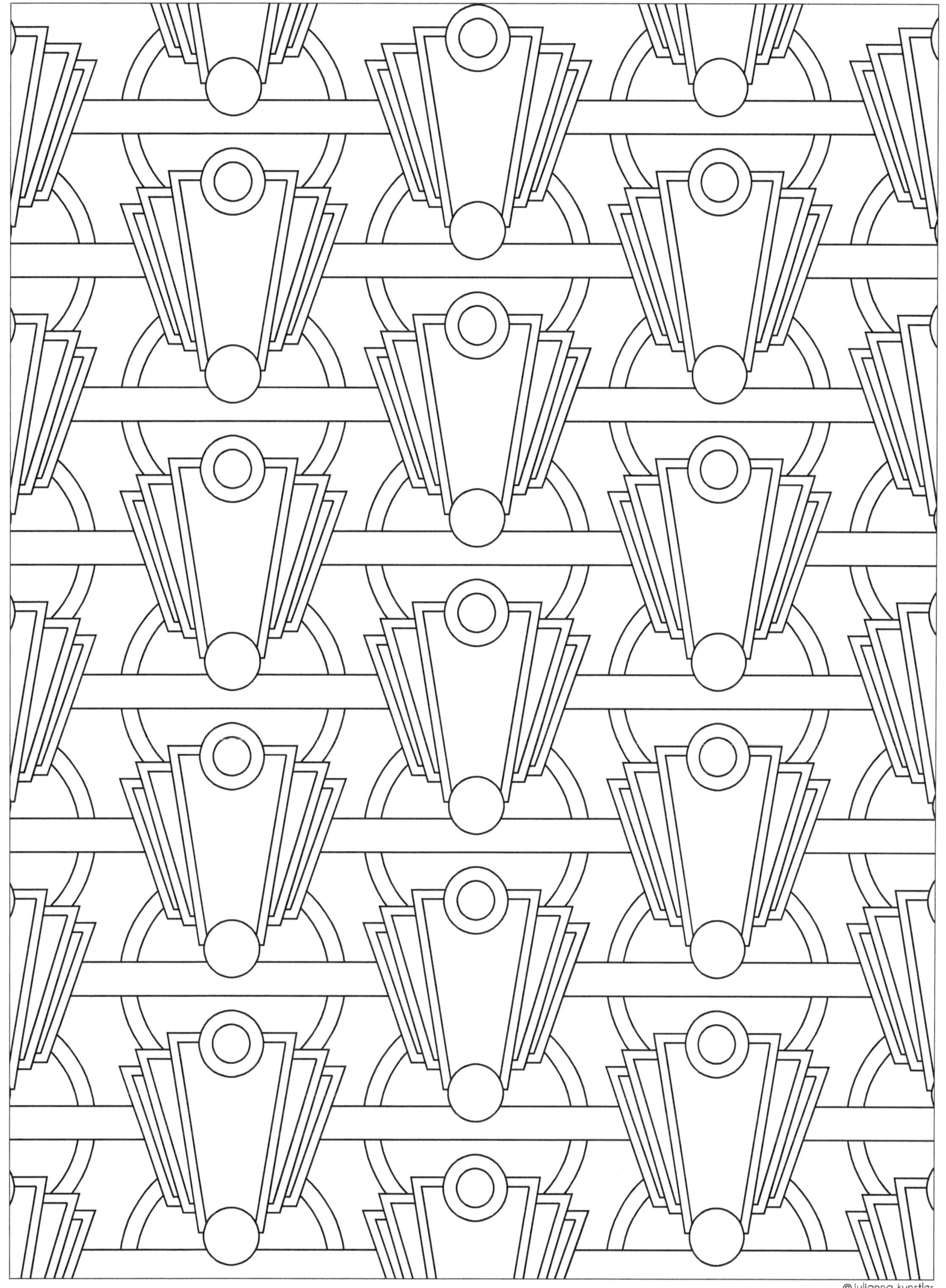

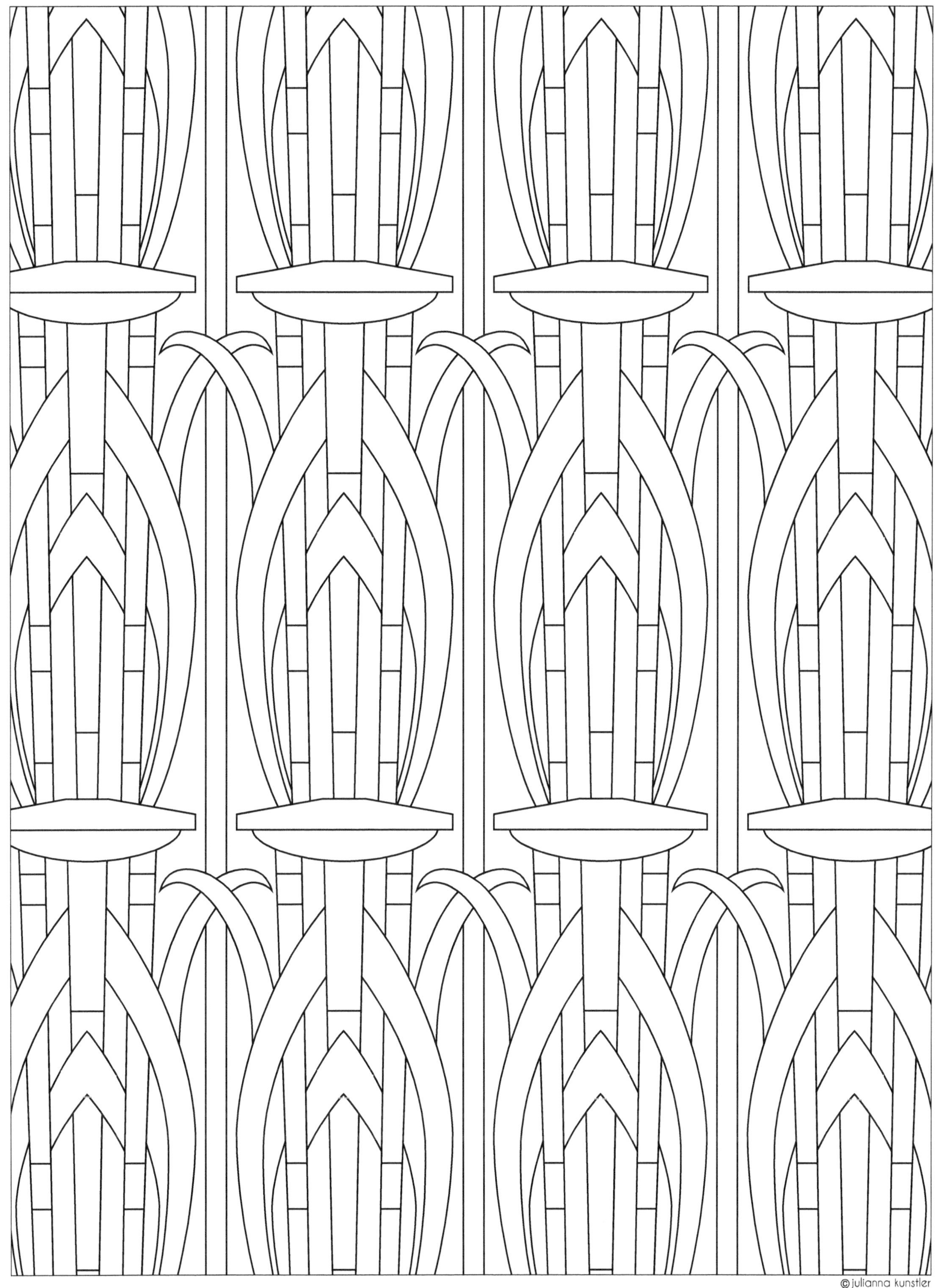

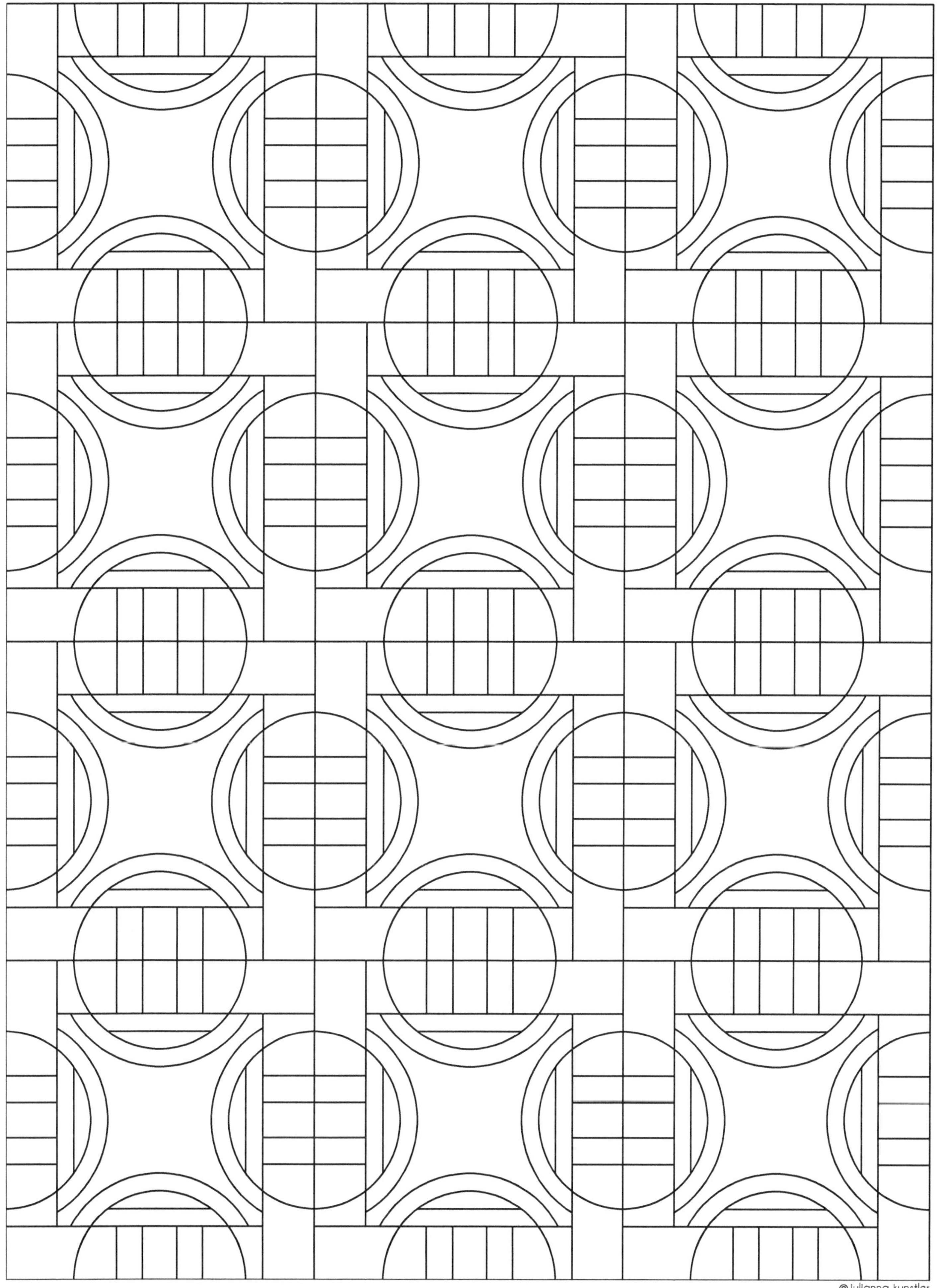

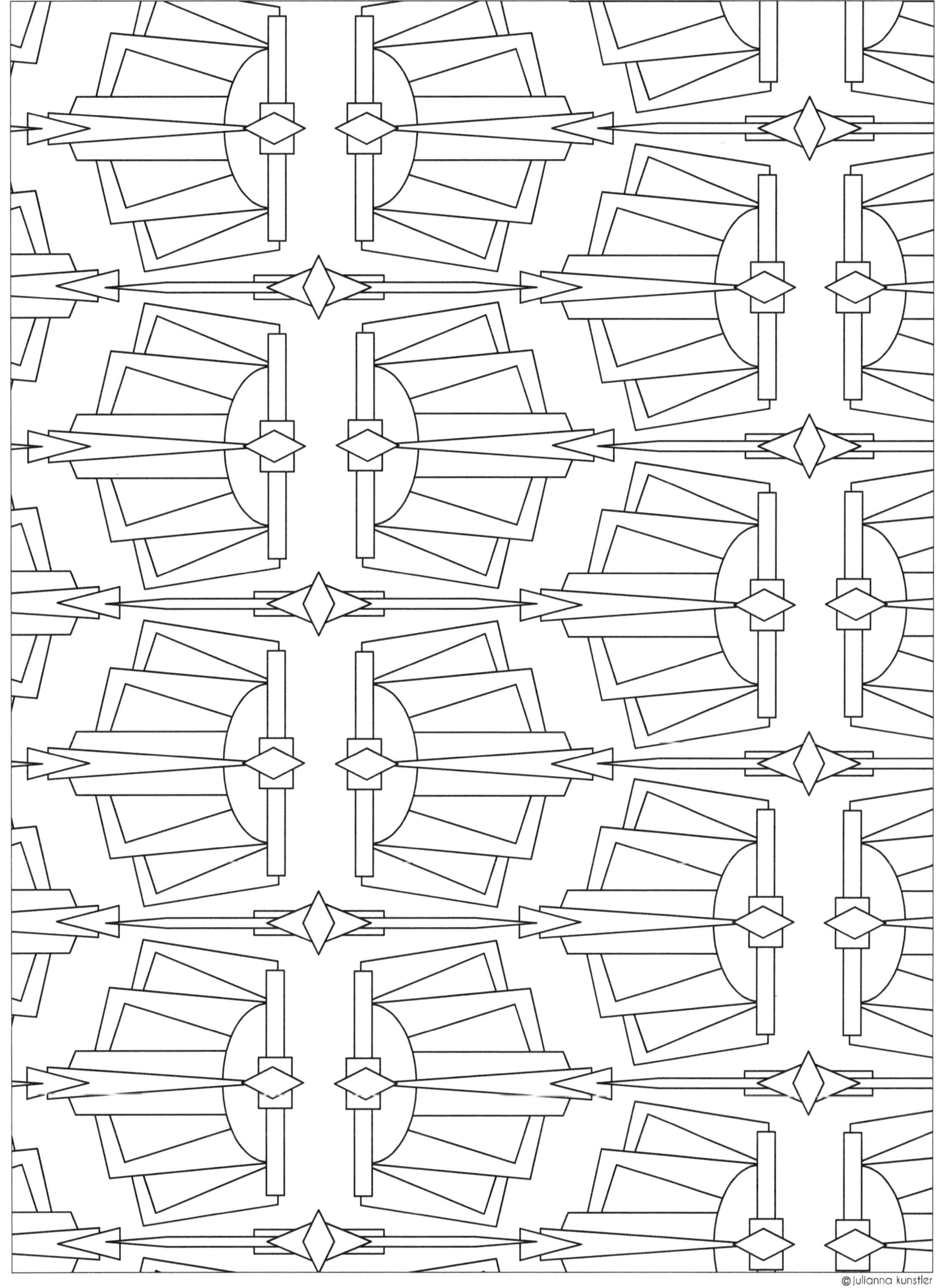

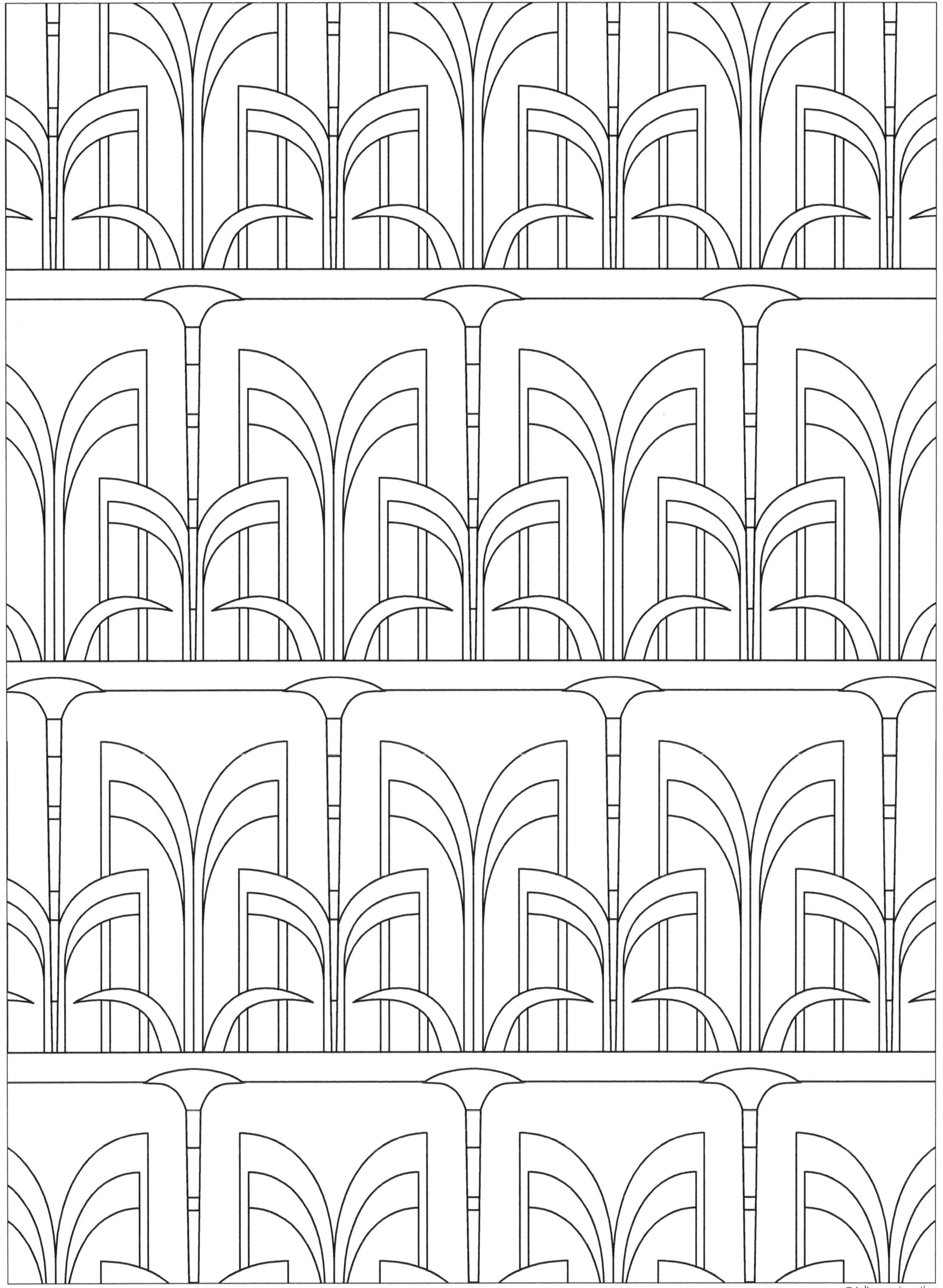

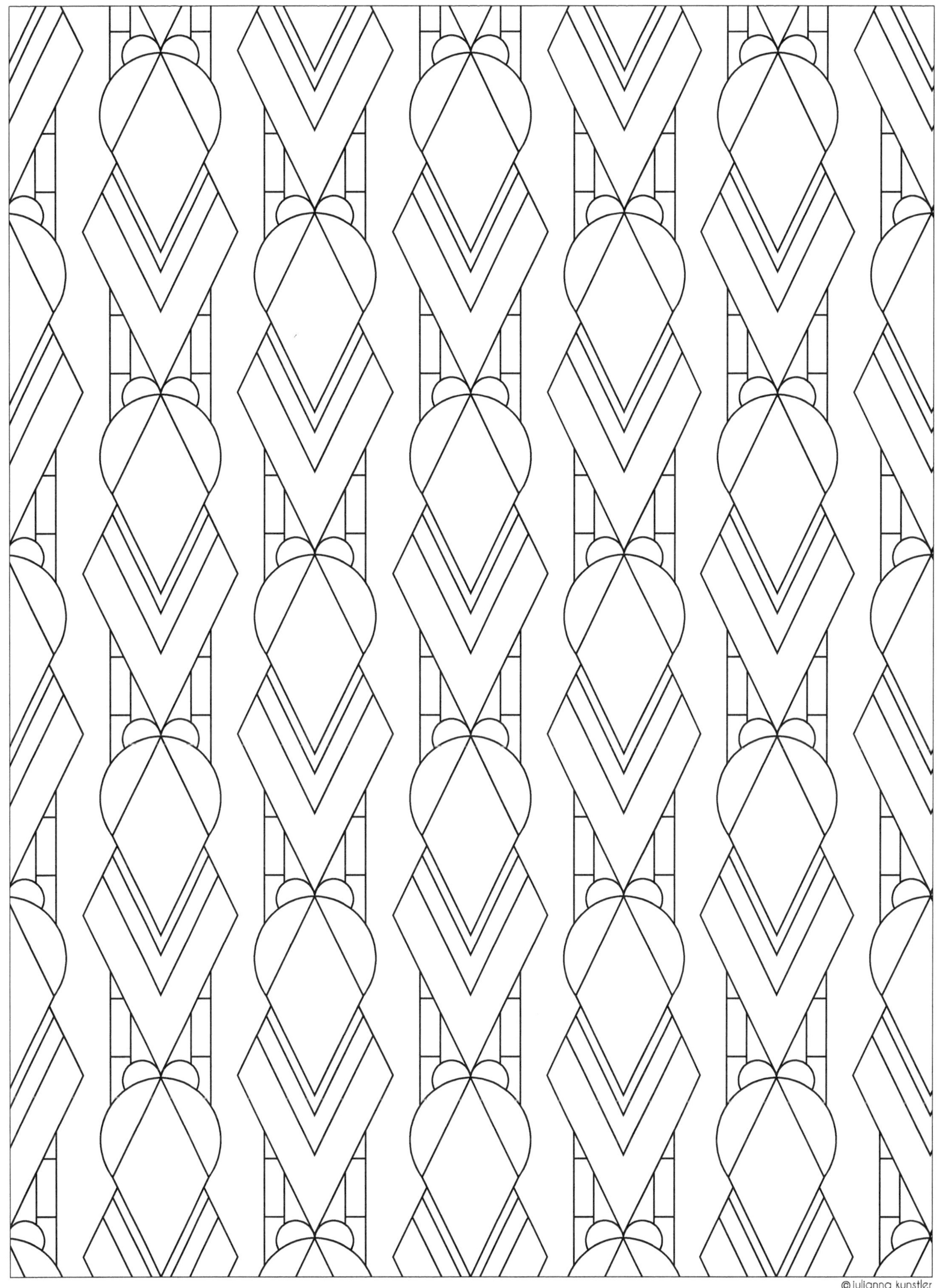

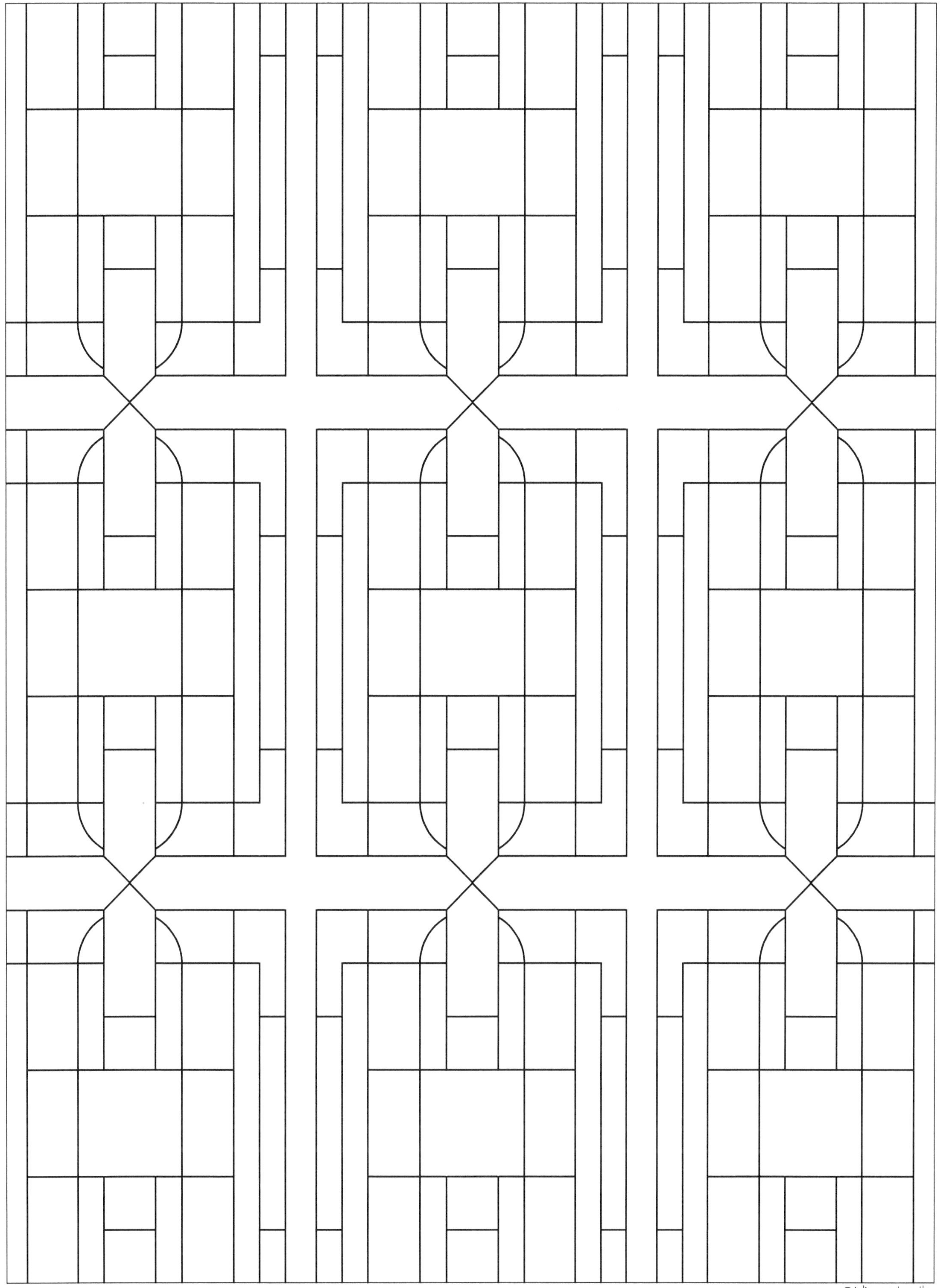

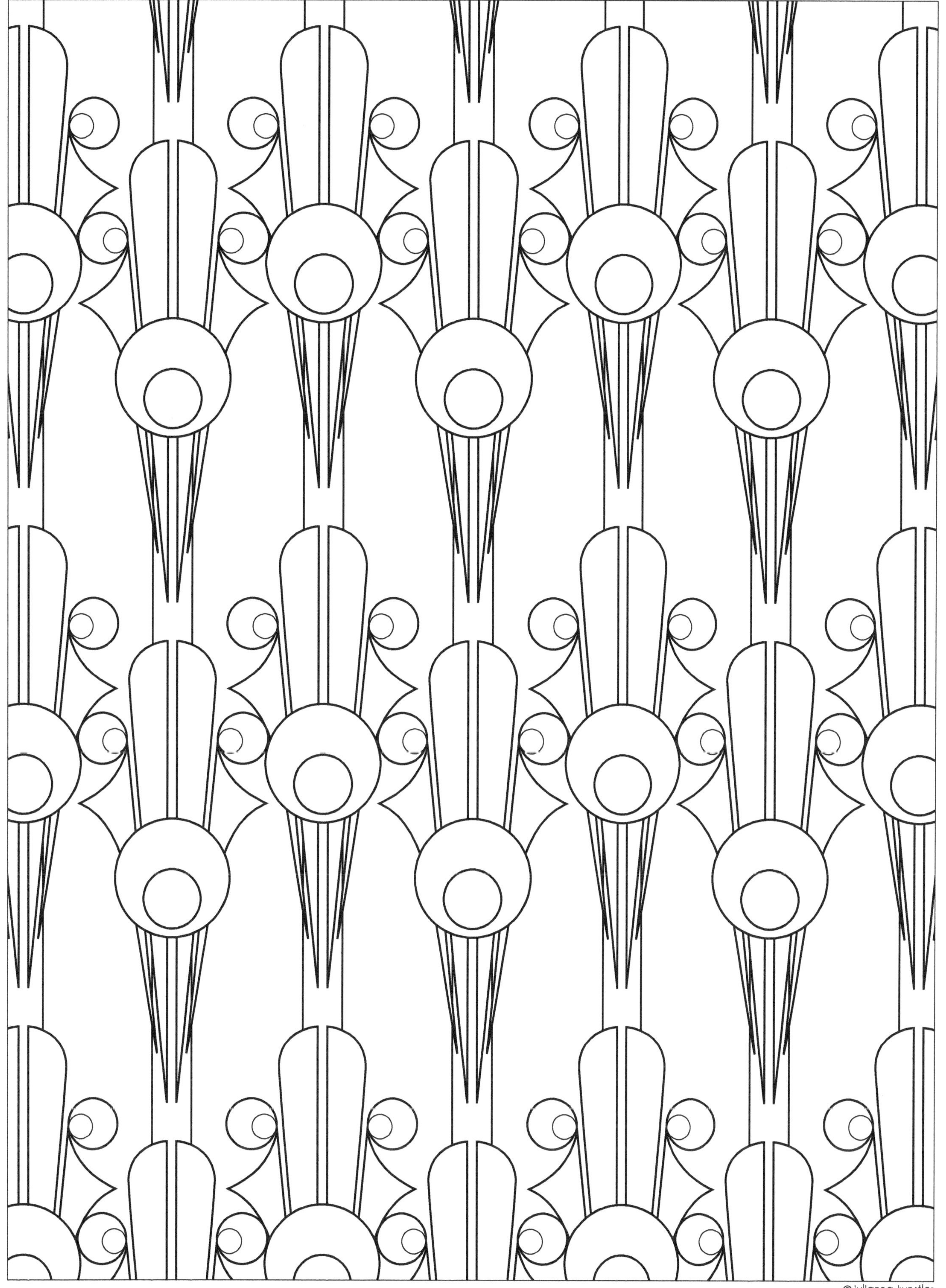

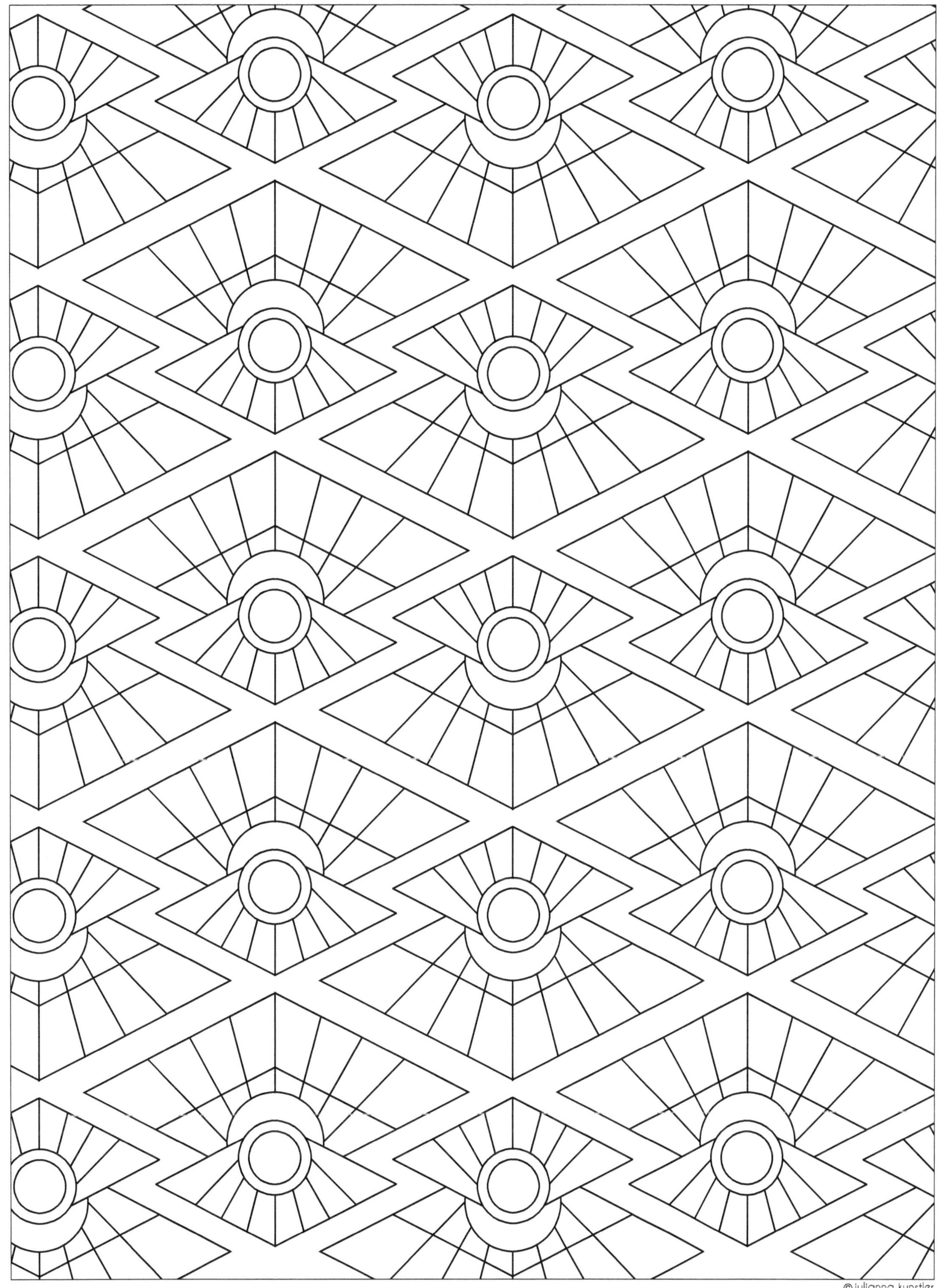

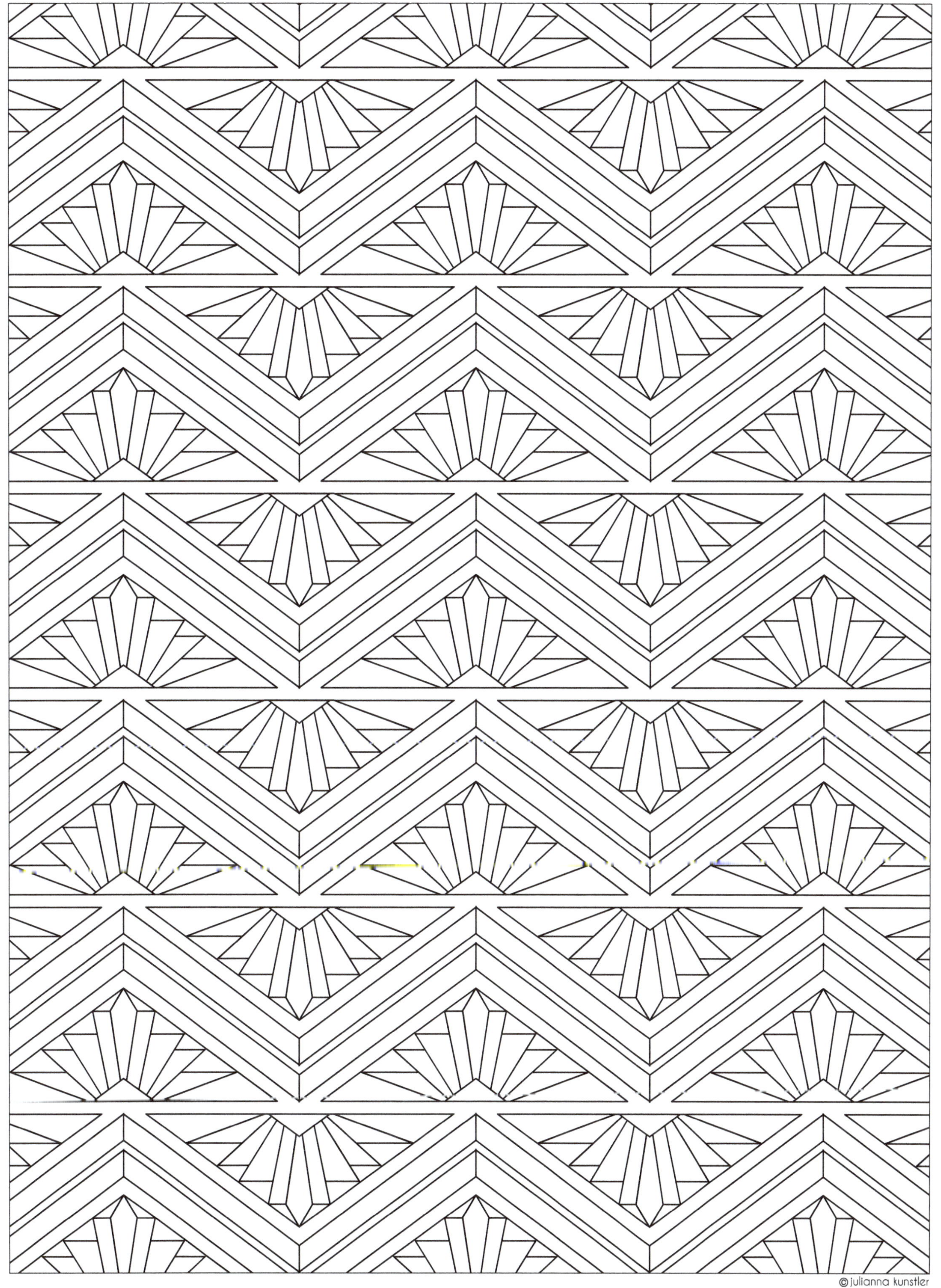

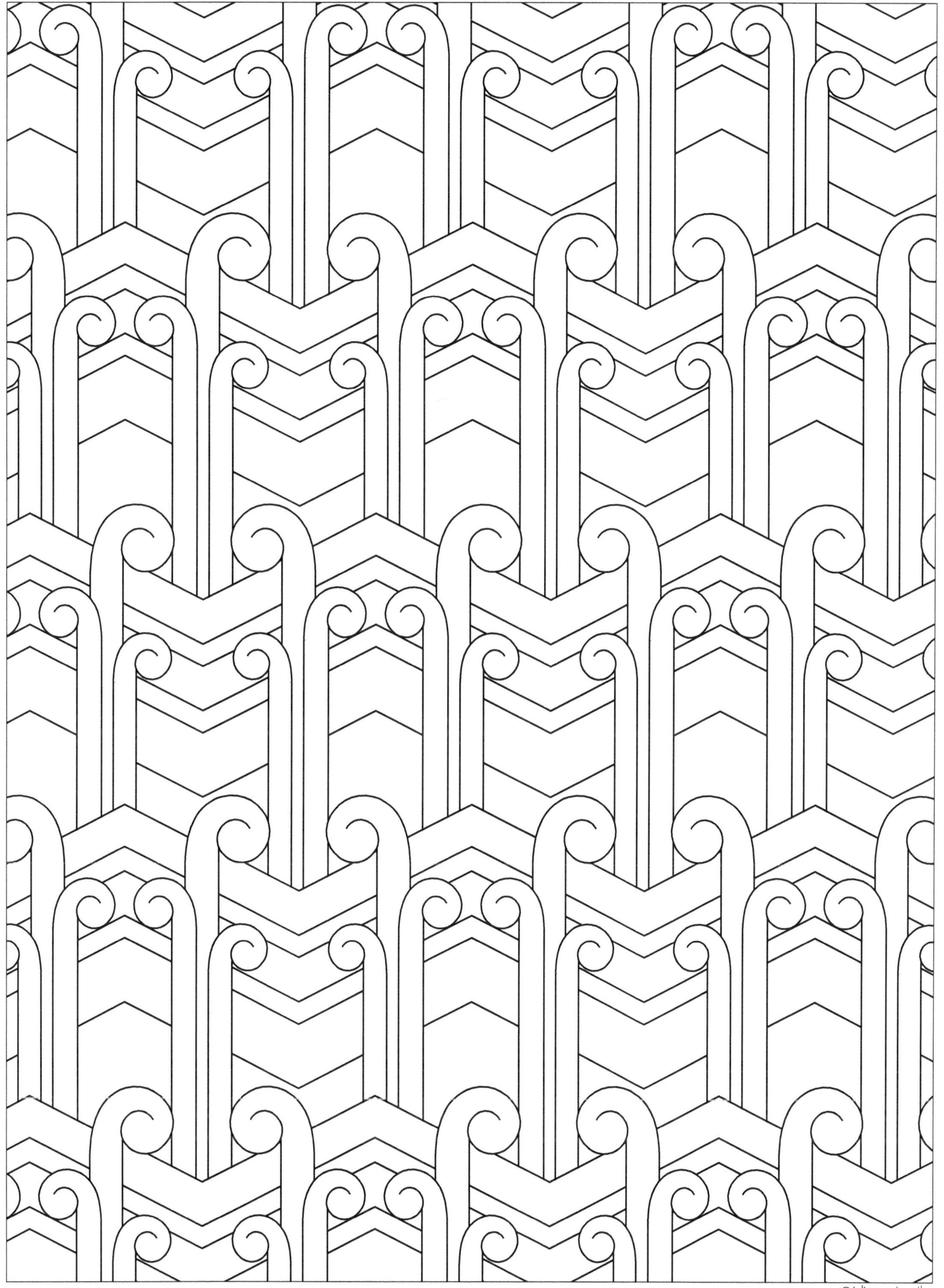

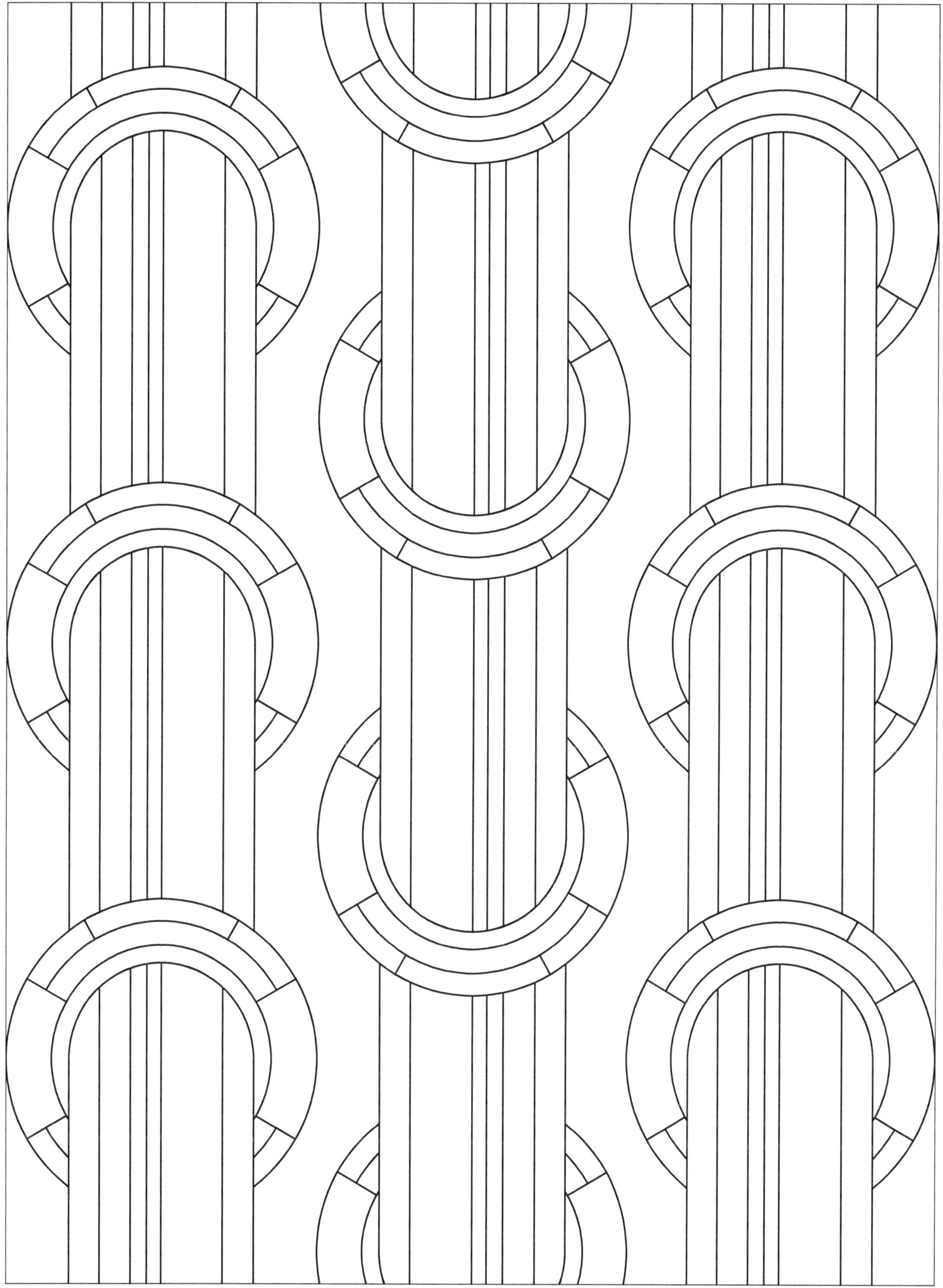

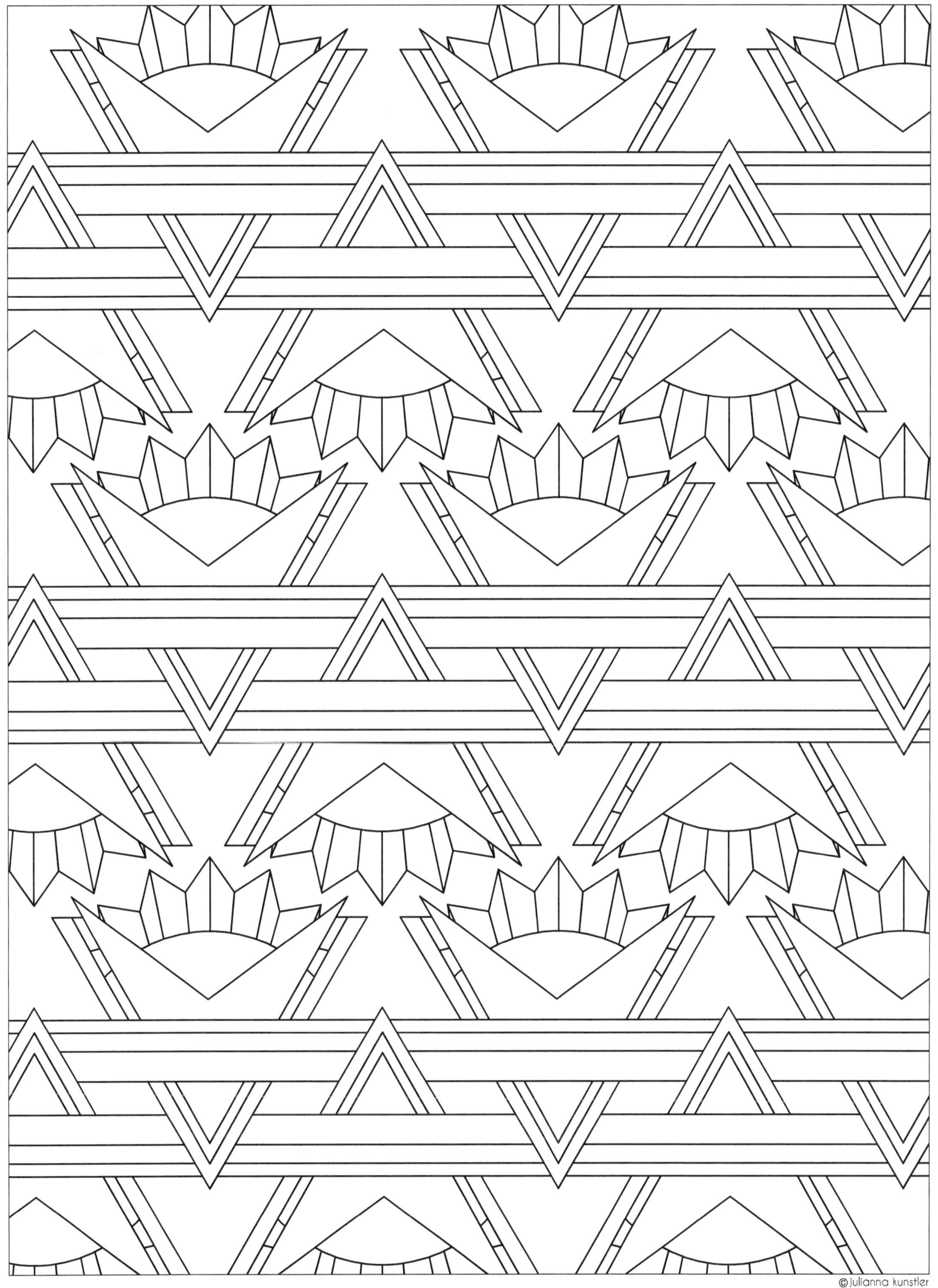

www.ingramcontent.com/pod-product-compliance
Lightning Source LLC
LaVergne TN
LVHW081424110826
845149LV00010B/1858

* 9 7 8 0 9 9 7 6 1 7 5 1 1 *